ALVIN KAMARA

Kerrily Sapet

BLUE Banner BIOGRAPHIES

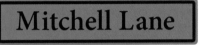

PUBLISHERS

mitchelllane.com

2001 SW 31st Avenue
Hallandale, FL 33009

First Edition, 2021.
Author: Kerrily Sapet
Designer: Ed Morgan
Editor: Morgan Brody

Series: Blue Banner Biographies
Title: Alvin Kamara / by Kerrily Sapet

Hallandale, FL : Mitchell Lane Publishers, [2021]

Library bound ISBN: 978-1-68020-617-3
eBook ISBN: 978-1-68020-618-0

Contents

Give Up or Grow Up

ALVIN KAMARA was lucky. When his mom bailed him out of jail at 3:00 a.m., she wasn't mad. She just looked at her 19-year-old son and asked, "What's next?" Alvin, one of the country's best high school football players, had been arrested in his hometown for driving without a license. The police officer lectured him: *Is this what you want to do? No kids will look up to you.* Other prisoners questioned him: *What are you doing here?* After spending eight hours in jail, Alvin was asking himself the same questions.

Alvin Kamara

Six months before, Alvin's future seemed certain. He planned to be a star on the University of Alabama's legendary football team and then play professionally in the NFL (National Football League). Then everything went wrong.

Before Alvin played his first college game, he injured his knee during training camp. He returned to practice after having surgery but was out for his freshman season. Sitting on the sidelines, Alvin grew frustrated and angry. "I think he felt like he let himself down a little bit and didn't reach the goals he set," said Mark Hocke, a coach at Alabama. "He felt like he had failed."

Unable to play the sport he loved, Alvin got in trouble. He set off fireworks on campus and loafed at practice. His coach set up "The Box"—four cones on the sidelines—where Alvin did push-ups and sit-ups as a punishment during practice. After getting suspended from the team twice, Alvin ditched school and headed home.

Alvin's arrest made him realize it was time to give up or grow up. "There was stuff that didn't work out like I wanted it to," he said. "I just knew I didn't want to stop [playing football]. I still believed I could do it, reach my dreams."

Alvin's coaches and family encouraged him to stay at the University of Alabama, but Alvin trusted his instincts. "I'm the type of person, I trust my gut, and when I get a feeling about something, I make a move based off of that," Alvin said.

Alvin packed one suitcase and moved to Hutchinson Community College in Kansas. At Hutchinson, away from a big team and big expectations, Alvin concentrated on school and football. His dedication and focus would help him achieve his dream of playing in the NFL.

Alvin Kamara believes everything happens for a reason. He is grateful for his difficult college years. Overcoming those challenges helped him become the person he is today—someone who works hard to be his best on and off the field.

Georgia's Mr. Football

ALVIN **MENTIAN KAMARA** was born on July 25, 1995 in Norcross, Georgia. His mother, Adama Kamara was from Liberia, a country in West Africa. She immigrated to the United States in 1989, before the First Liberian Civil War started. Adama was a single parent, raising Alvin and his sister, Garmai, by herself. Garmai, who was ten years old when Alvin was born, acted like his second parent. She drove Alvin to school and told him it was important to listen to his feelings and to be himself.

The small family struggled at times. Adama taught her children to work hard. She also encouraged them to trust their instincts, like she did when she fled Liberia to start a new life.

"My mom, she's got a different perspective on a lot of things just because of that foreign background," Alvin said. "It's just a lot of wisdom that you don't hear from a typical American."

When Alvin was in third grade, he started playing football like his friends. Alvin didn't like it though and quit. Two years later, he tried again. "They put the ball in my hands, and everything just took off from there," Alvin said.

Alvin loved the game. He practiced and played hard. Alvin could race down the field, leap into the air, and make incredible catches. He had excellent balance and quick feet to avoid getting tackled.

Alvin's early interest paid off as an All-America player in 2013.

"The first time he touched the ball as a tenth grader, I knew he was special," said Keith Maloof, Alvin's high school coach.

As a running back for his high school team, the Blue Devils, Alvin's job was to catch short passes, run with the ball, and score touchdowns. In his senior year, Alvin ran 2,264 yards, caught 22 passes, and scored 31 touchdowns. He helped his high school win its first state championship. One of the greatest high school football players in Georgia's history, Alvin was named Georgia's Mr. Football by the National Football Foundation.

As a talented running back, Alvin catches a pass during a practice for the Champion Gridiron Kings 7-on-7 football tournament at ESPN's Wide World of Sports in 2012.

Alvin runs for yardage during the second half of the Under Armour All-America high school football game in 2013.

Alvin received scholarship offers to universities with the best football programs in the country. Recruiters from the University of Alabama sent him 105 letters in one day. Alvin chose to attend the University of Alabama in the fall of 2013. He would play for the school's famous football team—the Crimson Tide.

Sunshine and Snow

AT THE **UNIVERSITY OF ALABAMA,** in Tuscaloosa, Alabama, Alvin Kamara practiced with the football team under the hot sun. His tough coach, Nick Saban, had sent more players to the pros than any other coach. Kamara faced fierce competition from his teammates. Three other running backs—all future NFL players—already played for Alabama.

Kamara played for the University of Alabama before he was injured.

Kamara's time at the University of Alabama was short. A pre-season knee injury forced him to sit on the sidelines. Discouraged, upset, and away from home for the first time, Kamara got into trouble and was suspended from the team.

Kamara took a chance. He left Alabama and enrolled at Hutchinson Community College in Kansas—a part of the United States he'd never even seen. The coach of the school's football team, the Blue Dragons, realized Kamara needed a second chance.

"Alvin was pretty quick to own his immaturity and his mistakes," Coach Rian Rhoades said. "Kids are going to make mistakes, and when they're willing to own them, to me, that says a lot about them."

That fall, Kamara played on Hutchinson's small football team. In the winter, he trudged to class in the snow—something he'd never seen growing up in the South—and worked out in the school's tiny weight room. Kamara learned from the mistakes he made at the University of Alabama. He focused on going to classes, studying, and playing football. Kamara became more mature and grew stronger.

After one year at Hutchinson, Kamara was ready for the fierce competition and the pressure of playing for a top college football team. He wanted to prove his talent to himself and others. Fans, reporters, and other players had criticized Kamara for his trouble at Alabama. They had called him names and said he wasn't good enough to play for a big team.

"All of the negativity is nothing but motivation," Kamara said. "I can honestly say I've never felt this compelled to succeed in my life. And succeed I will."

Kamara turned the negativity from his time at
Alabama to positive motivation.

Kamara transferred to the University of Tennessee. He spent the next two years proving himself on and off the football field. In his first game at Tennessee, he scored two touchdowns. Kamara's success continued and he became a respected team leader.

Kamara learned that he played best when he was being himself. He styled his hair in dreadlocks, sported a nose ring, and wore gold teeth in his mouth when he played. When Kamara was comfortable, he seemed unbeatable.

By the end of two seasons at the University of Tennessee, Kamara was one of the best college running backs in the country. He decided he was ready to play at the next level and declared himself eligible for the 2017 NFL Draft. He was listening to his instincts again—and NFL teams were waiting for him.

Kamara (*left*) carries the ball as Bowling Green linebacker Trenton Green attempts a tackle during a college football game in Nashville 2015.

Rookie in New Orleans

AS THE NFL draft approached, Kamara attended practices with several NFL teams. He jumped farther and higher than any other running back, sliced through arm tackles, and raced down the field. Kamara also aced a test predicting his ability to solve problems and perform under pressure.

Some NFL scouts suggested Kamara cut his hair and remove his nose ring because his appearance might concern teams. Kamara refused. He wanted to look the way he felt most comfortable.

Kamara runs a drill at the NFL Football Scouting Combine in Indianapolis, Friday, March 3, 2017.

"You can show a lie to a certain extent," Kamara said. "You can be somebody you're not to a certain extent. But soon enough, you've got to reveal who you are."

On April 28, 2017, the New Orleans Saints picked Kamara in the third round of the draft. He signed his contract to play for the Saints for four years. Kamara moved to New Orleans and began practicing with the team.

Kamara also started studying his team's playbook. It contained hundreds of plays written in a coded mishmash of words that gave the players directions. Kamara needed to remember plays like *Gun Flex Right Stack 394 Dragon Smoke Kill Turbo Sucker Right*.

On September 11, 2017, Kamara made his NFL debut in a game against the Minnesota Vikings. Two weeks later, he scored his first NFL touchdown, helping the Saints beat the Carolina Panthers. When Kamara won the Player of the Week award, he thanked his teammates with a surprise meal of barbecued ribs in their lockers.

"The kid's got it, man," said Jimmy Graham of the Green Bay Packers. "He's mentally strong. He leads by example and encourages people. It's pretty cool to see so young."

By the end of Kamara's first season, he had run more yards than any other NFL rookie running back ever and led all rookies with 81 catches and 14 touchdowns. Kamara was named to the Pro Bowl team. In February 2018, he received the NFL Rookie of the Year award.

Rookie in New Orleans

People in New Orleans loved Kamara. They wore fake dreadlocks and nose rings to games in his honor. He walked home to his apartment after games, stopping to chat with fans or to dine on famous New Orleans foods—beignets, grilled oysters, and spicy chicken wings. Kamara was comfortable being himself in his new city. "There's a whole lot of love here," he said. "There's a feel-good vibe." To Kamara, New Orleans was becoming home.

Kamara jumps into the stands to celebrate after a touchdown against the Washington Redskins in New Orleans in 2017.

CHAPTER FIVE

Superstar for the Saints

AFTER ALVIN KAMARA'S spectacular first season with the New Orleans Saints, he continued training. During the off-season, he worked to build up his leg strength and endurance. He also relaxed—treating himself to a strawberry peanut butter smoothie after his workouts, going out with friends, playing video games, and watching Disney movies—*The Lion King* and *The Little Mermaid*.

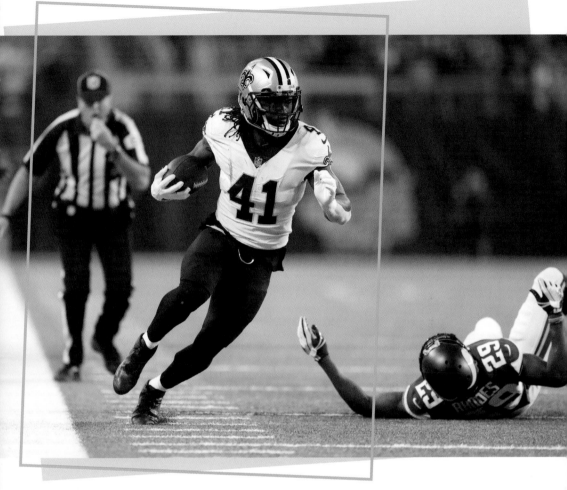

Kamara runs past Minnesota Vikings cornerback Xavier Rhodes during a playoff game in Minneapolis in January 2018.

When the 2018 season started, Kamara proved he could top his last season's success. He became the first player in NFL history to have 1,000 rushing yards and 1,000 receiving yards. He scored three touchdowns in one game and tied a record for scoring the most touchdowns in one season.

Kamara receives a handoff from quarterback Drew Brees during a game against the Atlanta Falcons in September 2018.

"He [Kamara] can do a lot of things," said Drew Brees. "He just plays with a lot of confidence, plays with a lot of swagger, but I think he also knows when it's time to work, knows when it's time to have fun."

Kamara did have fun. When he mentioned that his favorite candy was Airheads taffy, the company sent him so many Airheads that he built a throne out of candy boxes. The company even created a special flavor—Alvin Kamara Watermelon Zoom—for Kamara to hand out during games.

Even with Kamara's fame and success, he tries to remember what is important to him and who he is. "I don't just play football," he said. "I'm Alvin. Alvin Kamara. I happen to play football." When Kamara received a $1,000,000.00 bonus to continue playing with the Saints, he celebrated by getting some chicken wings.

Kamara wanted to use some of his money to help others. He remembered that growing up with a single parent was difficult. At Thanksgiving, Kamara gave away 800 turkeys to families in New Orleans. He also started a football camp to teach and inspire kids. At the end of camp, Kamara threw a pizza party and gave everyone new football cleats.

"Whatever dreams you have, whatever goals you have, you can realize them," Kamara told the kids. "I'm living breathing proof."

Alvin Kamara, superstar running back for the New Orleans Saints, is just starting his career. He has found a city and a team he loves in New Orleans. To Alvin Kamara, life is all about working hard, trusting your instincts, and being yourself. It's what makes him a success both on and off the football field.

Kamara runs against the Los Angeles Rams
during a game in January 2019.

Timeline

1995 Alvin Mentian Kamara is born in Norcross, Georgia.

2013 Kamara leads his high school to a state football championship; he begins attending the University of Alabama; he injures his knee.

2014 Kamara transfers to Hutchinson Community College in Kansas.

2015 Kamara attends the University of Tennessee; he becomes one of the top running backs in the country.

2017 Kamara is selected by the New Orleans Saints in the NFL draft.

2018 Kamara is named the NFL Rookie of the Year.

Career Stats

Total Games Played	31
Total Games Won	24
Total Games Lost	7
Total Touchdowns Scored	22
Total Yards Gained	3,146 yards
Total Receptions	182
Total Fumbles	1

Find Out More

Articles

Babb, Ken. "Alvin Kamara's Most Important Stop on the Way to NFL Stardom was a Kansas Community College." *The Washington Post*, August 15, 2018. https://www.washingtonpost.com/sports/highschools/alvin-kamaras-most-important-stop-on-way-to-nfl-stardom-was-a-kansas-community-college/2018/08/15/9c021b6c-9ff0-11e8-93e3-24d1703d2a7a_story.html?noredirect=on&utm_term=.cdf6d515baa9

Ledbetter, D. Orlando. "Alvin Kamara Named NFL Rookie of the Year." *The Atlanta Journal-Constitution*, February 2, 2018. https://www.ajc.com/sports/football/alvin-kamara-named-nfl-rookie-the-year/0IWvXyQ6p6bMfBoJHcPZqN/

On the Internet

Alvin Kamara Website
http://akamara41.com/my-story/

Alvin Kamara Stats
https://www.neworleanssaints.com/team/players-roster/alvin-kamara/

Alvin Kamara Details, News, and Videos
https://www.espn.com/nfl/player/_/id/3054850/alvin-kamara

Works Consulted

Canavan, Tom. "Alvin Kamara Runs for Three Second-Half TDs." AP News, September 30, 2018. https://apnews.com/ dd33bff56c864713b3448727033c0ea7

Erickson, Joel A. "A Gut Feeling Led Alvin Kamara From Alabama to Tennessee – Then Good Fortune Led Him to the Saints." *The New Orleans Advocate*, November 11, 2017. https://www.nola.com/sports/ saints/article_ddfc4d2b-4e2d-5cac-88d4-f5f7804657e9.html

Maya, Adam. "Saints RB Still Looking to 'Prove' Himself." NFL.com, June 16, 2019. http://www.nfl.com/news/story/0ap3000001033969/article/ saints-rb-alvin-kamara-still-looking-to-prove-himself

New Orleans Saints website. https://www.neworleanssaints.com

Parks, James. "Alvin Kamara Breaks Another NFL All-Time Record." 247Sports.com, October 2, 2018. https://247sports.com/nfl/new-, orleans-saints/Article/Alvin-Kamara-NFL-record-122803935/Amp/

Reid, Jason. "Tennessee's Alvin Kamara Takes an Unexpected Path to the NFL." *The Undefeated*, April 25, 2017. https://theundefeated.com/ features/tennessee-alvin-kamara-2017-nfl-draft/

Sigler, John. "Alvin Kamara Hosts Youth Football Camp at Saints Practice Facility." *USA Today*, June 1, 2019. https://saintswire.usatoday. com/2019/06/01/alvin-kamara-youth-football-camp-saints-practice-facility/

Triplett, Mike. "Alvin Kamara Somehow Finds Another Gear to Start Year 2." ESPN, September 15, 2018. https://www.espn.com/blog/new-orleans-saints/post/_/id/30466/alvin-kamara-somehow-finds-another-gear-to-start-year-2

Triplett, Mike. "Saints' Alvin Kamara has 'Good Anxiety' and his Football IQ Shows It." ESPN, June 19, 2019. https://www.espn.com/blog/new-orleans-saints/post/_/id/31997/saints-alvin-kamara-has-good-anxiety-and-his-football-iq-shows-it

"Saints' Alvin Kamara Lifts Up the Kids of New Orleans." yahoosports. com, November 14, 2018. https://sports.yahoo.com/saints-alvin-kamara-lifts-kids-new-orleans-110525681.html

Index

About the Author

Kerrily Sapet is the author of over 25 books for children and multiple magazine articles. Growing up in Pittsburgh, Pennsylvania, she was surrounded by Pittsburgh Steelers fans and attended Pennsylvania State University, home of the Nittany Lions. Sapet lives near Chicago, Illinois and, unlike Alvin Kamara, loves snowy, Midwestern winters.